Orange **Line 3**

Vokabellernheft Erweiterungskurs

Ernst Klett Verlag
Stuttgart • Leipzig

Vorwort

Dieses Vokabellernheft im Taschenformat enthält alle Wörter und Wendungen aus *Orange Line* 3 Erweiterungskurs.
Aufgrund seines praktischen Formats kannst du es überall hin mitnehmen, um deine Wörter zu lernen und zu wiederholen.
Am besten hast du beim Lernen immer einen Bleistift zur Hand. Damit markierst du Wörter und Wendungen, die dir besondere Schwierigkeiten bereiten. Diese kannst du dann in regelmäßigen Abständen immer wieder durchgehen.
Am Ende jeder Unit findest du zahlreiche Übungen, mit denen du das Gelernte wiederholen, ordnen und dich auf Vokabeltests vorbereiten kannst.

Viel Spaß wünscht dir dein *Orange-Line*-Team!

Unit 1 What's your game?

Check-in

home [həʊm]	Heimat
rugby ['rʌgbi]	Rugby
century ['sentʃri]	Jahrhundert
each [i:tʃ]	jede/jeder/jedes
its [ɪts]	sein/seine; ihr/ihre
American football [əˌmerɪkən 'fʊtbɔ:l]	Football
player ['pleɪə]	Spieler/Spielerin, Mitspieler/Mitspielerin
helmet ['helmət]	Helm
during (+ noun) ['djʊərɪŋ]	während (+ Nomen)
to catch, caught, caught [kætʃ, kɔ:t, kɔ:t]	fangen, erreichen
stadium ['steɪdiəm]	Stadion
you [ju:; jə]	man
to learn [lɜ:n]	erfahren
at the back [ət ðə 'bæk]	im hinteren Teil, hinten
at the front [ət ðə 'frʌnt]	im vorderen Teil, vorne
to bat [bæt]	schlagen
bat [bæt]	Schläger
glove [glʌv]	Handschuh
rugby boot [ˌrʌgbi 'bu:t]	Rugbyschuh, Stollenschuh
baseball ['beɪsbɔ:l]	Baseball
batter ['bætə]	Schlagmann/Schlagfrau
to score [skɔ:]	punkten, ein Tor schießen
run [rʌn]	Run, Runde
action ['ækʃn]	Handlung, Aktion
stand [stænd]	Tribüne
against [ə'genst]	gegen
competition [ˌkɒmpə'tɪʃn]	Wettbewerb, Turnier

Language

pitch [pɪtʃ]	Spielfeld

national ['næʃnl]	landesweit
best [best]	am besten
beach [bi:tʃ]	Strand
net [net]	Netz
across [ə'krɒs]	über, hinüber, quer durch/ darüber
court [kɔ:t]	Spielfeld
sand [sænd]	Sand
goalkeeper ['gəʊlˌki:pə]	Torwart
back line [ˌbæk 'lain]	Grundlinie
to **kill** [kɪl]	töten; hier: tot machen
signal ['sɪgnl]	Zeichen
full (of) [fʊl]	ganz, voll (von/mit)
birth [bɜ:θ]	Geburt
height [haɪt]	Höhe, Größe
weight [weɪt]	Gewicht
foot, feet (pl) [fʊt; fi:t]	Fuß (Längenmaß: 30,48 cm)
inch [ɪnʃ]	Zoll (Längenmaß: 2,54 cm)
gramme (g) [græm]	Gramm
stone [stəʊn]	brit. Gewichtseinheit (= 6,35 kg)
union ['ju:njən]	Liga; Vereinigung, Union
was/were born [bɔ:n]	wurde(n) geboren
about [ə'baʊt]	ungefähr, circa, etwa
couch potato ['kaʊtʃ pəˌteɪtəʊ]	Stubenhocker
couch [kaʊtʃ]	Couch, Sofa
to **cycle** ['saɪkl]	Rad fahren
secretary ['sekrətri]	Sekretär/Sekretärin
firm [fɜ:m]	Firma
racing ['reɪsɪŋ]	Renn-
boss [bɒs]	Boss, Chef/Chefin
walk [wɔ:k]	Spaziergang
active ['æktɪv]	aktiv
enough [ɪ'nʌf]	genug, genügend
you see [jʊ 'si:]	weißt du
to **imagine** [ɪ'mædʒɪn]	sich (etwas) vorstellen
jersey ['dʒɜ:zi]	Trikot
pool [pu:l]	Schwimmbecken

swimsuit ['swɪmsu:t]	Badeanzug
tennis ['tenɪs]	Tennis
star [stɑ:]	Star, Stern
umpire ['ʌmpaɪə]	Schiedsrichter/Schiedsrichterin
half-time [ˌhɑ:f'taɪm]	Halbzeit
score [skɔ:]	Punktestand, Spielstand
referee [ˌrefr'i:]	Schiedsrichter/Schiedsrichterin
to **blow, blew, blown** [bləʊ, blu:, bləʊn]	blasen
whistle ['wɪsl]	Trillerpfeife
It's a draw. [ˌɪts‿ə 'drɔ:]	Es steht unentschieden.
swimming pool ['swɪmɪŋ ˌpu:l]	Schwimmbecken; Schwimmbad

Get fit!

talk [tɔ:k]	Vortrag, Rede
catcher ['kætʃə]	Fänger/Fängerin
base [beɪs]	Base
pitcher ['pɪtʃə]	Werfer/Werferin
home plate ['həʊm ˌpleɪt]	Home Plate
at the top [ət ðə 'tɒp]	oben, im oberen Teil
top [tɒp]	Spitze, oberer Teil
at the bottom [ət ðə 'bɒtəm]	unten, im unteren Teil
bottom ['bɒtəm]	Boden, Grund, unterer Teil
to **be missing** [bi: 'mɪsɪŋ]	fehlen

Overheard

row [rəʊ]	Reihe
half-price [ˌhɑ:f'praɪs]	zum halben Preis
to **send off** [send‿'ɒf]	vom Platz verweisen
British ['brɪtɪʃ]	britisch
cup [kʌp]	Tasse, Kelch; Pokal
BC (= before Christ) [bi:'si:]	vor Christus
goal post ['gəʊl pəʊst]	Torpfosten
post [pəʊst]	Pfosten, Mast

Facts and fiction

practice ['præktɪs]	Training
nearly ['nɪəli]	fast, annähernd
doorstep ['dɔ:step]	Türstufe
next door [ˌnekst 'dɔ:]	nebenan
ancient ['eɪnʃnt]	alt
to **moan** [məʊn]	(sich) (be)klagen
to **dig up, dug up, dug up** [dɪg‿'ʌp, dʌg‿'ʌp, dʌg‿'ʌp]	ausgraben
lonely ['ləʊnli]	einsam
to **feel sorry for** [fi:l 'sɒri]	Mitleid haben mit, bedauern
home-made [ˌhəʊm'meɪd]	selbst gemacht
well [wel]	gut
fight [faɪt]	Kampf
thick [θɪk]	dick (nicht für Personen); dumm
to **come down** [kʌm 'daʊn]	herunterkommen, sich legen
fair [feə]	gerecht, fair
not ... either [ˌnɒt ... 'aɪðə]	auch nicht
to **substitute** ['sʌbstɪtju:t]	auswechseln, ersetzen
instead of [ɪn'sted‿əv]	statt, anstatt
What a laugh! [ˌwɒt‿ə 'lɑ:f]	Wie lustig!
to **run into** [rʌn‿'ɪntə]	laufen gegen, stoßen gegen
to **knock out** [nɒk‿'aʊt]	k. o. schlagen, umhauen
himself [hɪm'self]	sich (selbst)
to **take off** [teɪk‿'ɒf]	wegbringen, fortschaffen
crowd [kraʊd]	Menschenmenge
rest [rest]	Rest
to **change your mind** [ˌtʃeɪndʒ jə 'maɪnd]	deine Meinung ändern

Wordwise

the same [seɪm]	derselbe/dieselbe/dasselbe; gleich

1 Sports

Ergänze die fehlenden Buchstaben.

1. r_gb_y
2. pla_e_
3. c_mp_t_t_on
4. st_d_um
5. p_ tc_
6. g_alk_ep_r
7. b_ck _ine
8. _e_e_ee

2 Nouns

Verbinde die Nomen richtig.

1. American	pool
2. rugby	post
3. back	football
4. couch	plate
5. swimming	line
6. home	boot
7. goal	potato

3 Baseball

Welche Wörter fallen dir zum Thema „Baseball" ein?

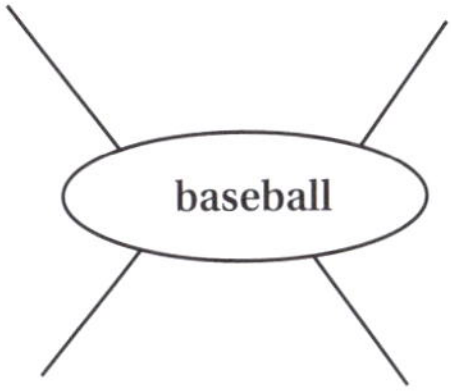

4 Odd one out

Welches Wort fällt aus der Reihe?

1.	court	stadium	cup
2.	catcher	doorstep	player
3.	umpire	referee	whistle
4.	century	inch	BC
5.	stand	height	weight
6.	birth	beach	sand
7.	helmet	glove	net
8.	fair	ancient	old

5 Prepositions

Finde die richtigen Präpositionen.

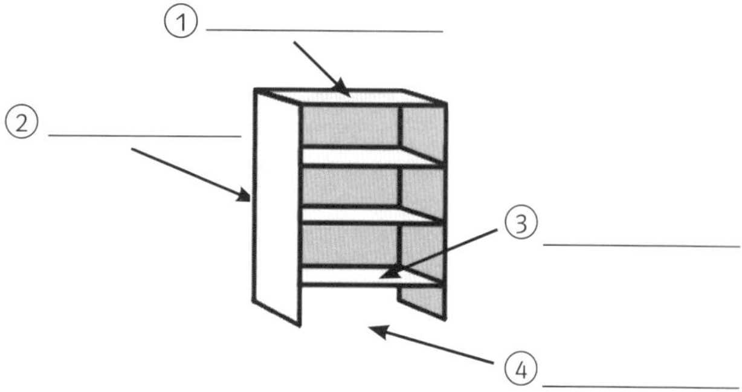

6 Little words

Wie heißen die kleinen Wörter?

1. während ____________
2. man ____________
3. gegen ____________
4. fast, annähernd ____________
5. genug ____________
6. über, hinüber ____________

7 Opposites

Finde das Gegenteil.

1. at the top ______________________
2. empty ______________________
3. new ______________________
4. at the front ______________________

8 Words for pictures

Finde die richtigen Wörter zu den Bildern.

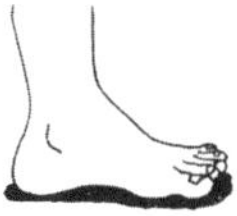

1. ______________________

2. ______________________

3. ______________________

4. ______________________

5. ______________________

9 Plurals

Wie lautet die Mehrzahl?

1. cup ____________________
2. century ____________________
3. pitch ____________________
4. foot ____________________
5. couch potato ____________________
6. boss ____________________

10 The letter 'o'

In diesen Wörtern kommt überall der Buchstabe „o" vor, aber er wird nicht immer gleich ausgesprochen. Sortiere die Wörter.

across	score	row	born	post	lonely
top	knock	home	glove	stone	

[əʊ] ____________________ ____________________

[ɒ] ____________________ ____________________

[ɔ:] ____________________ ____________________

[ʌ] ____________________ ____________________

11 Nouns from verbs

Bilde Nomen, indem du „-er“ an die Verben anhängst.

1. to catch ________________ 4. to play ________________

2. to bat ________________ 5. to teach ________________

3. to sing ________________ 6. to report ________________

12 Verbs

In dieser Unit hast du einige Verben zum Thema „Sport“ gelernt. Kannst du dich an alle erinnern? Schreibe sie auf.

____

____

____

13 Difficult words

Welche Wörter konntest du dir besonders gut merken?

____

____

Welche Wörter fallen dir noch schwer? Schreibe sie auf und wiederhole sie noch einmal.

____

____

Unit 2 Out and about in London

Check-in

capsule ['kæpsju:l]	Kapsel
spectacular [spek'tækjələ]	spektakulär
view [vju:]	Aussicht, Sicht
palace ['pælɪs]	Palast
royal ['rɔɪəl]	königlich
to **relive** [ˌri:'lɪv]	wieder erleben
great [greɪt]	groß
queue [kju:]	(Warte-)Schlange
traffic jam ['træfɪk ˌdʒæm]	Stau
traffic ['træfɪk]	Verkehr
Tube [tju:b]	Londoner U-Bahn
to **go far** [gəʊ 'fɑ:]	weit kommen, es weit bringen
trendy ['trendi]	modisch
to **build, built, built** [bɪld, bɪlt, bɪlt]	bauen
tower ['taʊə]	Turm
building ['bɪldɪŋ]	Gebäude
valuable ['væljuəbl]	wertvoll
jewel ['dʒu:əl]	Juwel
world [wɜ:ld]	Welt
crown [kraʊn]	Krone
underground ['ʌndəgraʊnd]	U-Bahn

Language

tourist ['tʊərɪst]	Tourist/Touristin
pickpocket ['pɪkˌpɒkɪt]	Taschendieb/Taschendiebin
local ['ləʊkl]	lokal, örtlich
newspaper ['nju:sˌpeɪpə]	Zeitung
to **change** [tʃeɪndʒ]	umsteigen
thanks to ['θæŋks tə]	dank (dir/ihnen), wegen
to **rob** [rɒb]	rauben, ausrauben
within [wɪ'ðɪn]	innerhalb

teenager ['ti:nˌeɪdʒə]	Teenager, Jugendlicher/ Jugendliche
busy ['bɪzi]	belebt
handbag ['hænbæg]	Handtasche
businessman, businessmen (pl) ['bɪznɪsmən; 'bɪznɪsmen]	Geschäftsmann
rucksack ['rʌksæk]	Rucksack
finally ['faɪnli]	endlich, schließlich
cathedral [kə'θi:drl]	Kathedrale, Dom
toy [tɔɪ]	Spielzeug
fine [faɪn]	Geldbuße, Geldstrafe
rich [rɪtʃ]	reich
one(s) [wʌn(z)]	(Platzhalter für ein Nomen)
to **become, became, become** [bɪ'kʌm, bɪ'keɪm, bɪ'kʌm]	werden
blond(e)-haired ['blɒndˌheəd]	blond
actress ['æktrəs]	Schauspielerin
model ['mɒdl]	Model, Modell
sporty ['spɔ:ti]	sportlich
prince [prɪns]	Prinz
souvenir [ˌsu:və'nɪə]	Souvenir, Andenken
millennium [mɪ'leniəm]	Jahrtausend
after ['ɑ:ftə]	nachdem
to **enter** ['entə]	sich beteiligen an; eintreten, betreten
landmark ['lændmɑ:k]	Wahrzeichen, Markstein
to **give up** [gɪv‿'ʌp]	aufgeben
article ['ɑ:tɪkl]	Artikel
to **come true** [kʌm 'tru:]	wahr werden
architect ['ɑ:kɪtekt]	Architekt/Architektin
rim [rɪm]	Radkranz
piece [pi:s]	Stück
to **complete** [kəm'pli:t]	vervollständigen
wheel [wi:l]	Rad
to **lift** [lɪft]	hochziehen, hochheben
to **add** [æd]	hinzufügen, addieren
platform ['plætfɔ:m]	Plattform, Tribüne, Bahnsteig

to **fix (to)** [fɪks]	befestigen, anbringen, reparieren
huge [hjuːdʒ]	riesig, gewaltig
to **design** [dɪ'zaɪn]	entwerfen; zeichnen
to **construct** [kən'strʌkt]	bauen, konstruieren
fortress ['fɔːtrəs]	Festung
prison ['prɪzn]	Gefängnis
menagerie [mə'nædʒri]	Menagerie
king [kɪŋ]	König
to **die** [daɪ]	sterben
wild [waɪld]	wild
to **marry** ['mæri]	heiraten
monastery ['mɒnəstri]	Kloster
university [ˌjuːnɪ'vɜːsəti]	Universität
exhibition [ˌeksɪ'bɪʃn]	Ausstellung, Vorführung

Get fit!

fifth [fɪfθ]	Fünftel
quarter ['kwɔːtə]	Viertel
to **destroy** [dɪ'strɔɪ]	zerstören
wood [wʊd]	Holz
straw [strɔː]	Stroh
baker ['beɪkə]	Bäcker/Bäckerin
to **put out** [pʊt‿'aʊt]	ausmachen; löschen
fire [faɪə]	Feuerstelle, Kaminfeuer
to **smell, smelt, smelt** [smel, smelt, smelt]	riechen
smoke [sməʊk]	Rauch
spark [spɑːk]	Funke(n)
flame [fleɪm]	Flamme
to **burn, burnt, burnt** [bɜːn, bɜːnt, bɜːnt]	(ver)brennen
for … [fɔː; fə]	… lang
fire brigade ['faɪə brɪˌgeɪd]	Feuerwehr
to **damage** ['dæmɪdʒ]	beschädigen
half [hɑːf]	Hälfte
boat [bəʊt]	Boot, Schiff
to **the country** [tʊ ðə 'kʌntri]	aufs Land

Overheard

meaning ['mi:nɪŋ]	Bedeutung
dialogue ['daɪəlɒg]	Dialog, Gespräch

Facts and fiction

to **train** [treɪn]	eine Ausbildung machen
gardener ['gɑ:dnə]	Gärtner/Gärtnerin
courier ['kʊriə]	Kurier
pollution [pə'lu:ʃn]	(Umwelt-)Verschmutzung
to **argue** ['ɑ:gju:]	streiten, argumentieren
to **carry** ['kæri]	befördern
tin [tɪn]	Dose, Büchse
sauerkraut ['saʊəkraʊt]	Sauerkraut
milkman, milkmen (pl) ['mɪlkmən; 'mɪlkmen]	Milchmann
round [raʊnd]	Runde
tradition [trə'dɪʃn]	Tradition
dairy ['deəri]	Molkerei
company ['kʌmpəni]	Gesellschaft, Firma; Kompanie
to **deliver** [dɪ'lɪvə]	liefern
at the crack of dawn [ˌkræk‿əv 'dɔ:n]	im Morgengrauen
customer ['kʌstəmə]	Kunde/Kundin
since [sɪnts]	seit, seitdem
taxi ['tæksi]	Taxi
like the back of my hand [laɪk ðə 'bæk‿əv maɪ ˌhænd]	wie meine Westentasche
kind [kaɪnd]	Art, Sorte
to **expect** [ɪk'spekt]	erwarten
punk [pʌŋk]	Punk
style [staɪl]	Stil; hier: Frisur
post office ['pəʊst‿ɒfɪs]	Postamt
regular ['regjələ]	Stammkunde/Stammkundin
to **get interested** [get 'ɪntrəstɪd]	sich interessieren
mess [mes]	Durcheinander

1 Adjectives

Setze die richtigen Adjektive ein.

scary trendy expensive spectacular rich

1. The views from the London Eye are ________________ .
2. The shops in London are very ________________ .
3. A lot of ________________ people live in London.
4. They can buy ________________ houses.
5. The London Dungeon is really ________________ .

2 Word puzzle

Finde die 14 Wörter im Puzzle. Sie sind senkrecht, waagerecht und diagonal versteckt.

after, busy, courier, finally, for, huge, jewel, newspaper, queue, prince, regular, royal, since, taxi

R	F	D	J	J	S	N	O	N	R
M	O	A	R	E	W	E	C	T	E
F	R	Y	K	W	F	W	O	P	G
C	L	F	A	E	B	S	U	R	U
T	A	X	I	L	U	P	R	I	L
H	S	I	N	C	E	A	I	N	A
B	U	S	Y	L	U	P	E	C	R
I	A	G	A	F	T	E	R	E	K
F	S	K	E	E	T	R	F	G	N
A	D	C	H	F	J	E	N	T	D
S	D	L	C	Q	U	E	U	E	H
F	I	N	A	L	L	Y	E	R	L

3 Odd one out

Welches Wort fällt aus der Reihe? Markiere es.

1. palace	crown	underground
2. tower	teenager	building
3. to enter	to design	to construct
4. spark	flame	capsule
5. milkman	dairy	sauerkraut

4 Buildings

Welche Gebäude kennst du?

5 Verbs

Verbinde die Wörter richtig.

1. to go	interested
2. to give	out
3. to come	far
4. to put	up
5. to get	true

6 In London

Ergänze die fehlenden Buchstaben.

1. b__il__i__g	5. tr__di__i__n
2. de__i__er	6 m__na__te__y
3. __ol__u__i__n	7. __tr__w
4. mi__km__n	8. f__rt__e__s

7 Comparisons

Setze die richtigen Wörter ein.

oldest faster trendiest scariest best

1. The London Dungeon is the ____________ museum in London.
2. You can get the ____________ views of London from the London Eye.
3. The Tube is ____________ than the bus.
4. Some of the ____________ shops are in the King's Road.
5. The Tower is one of the ____________ buildings in London.

8 Mixed up words

Welche Wörter sind hier durcheinander geraten?

1. weiv ____________
2. evlrie ____________
3. drneudonrug ____________
4. kpocicpket ____________

9 Little words

Wie heißen die kleinen Wörter?

1. innerhalb ______________
2. nachdem ______________
3. Viertel ______________
4. endlich ______________
5. seit, seitdem ______________

10 Adjectives

Wie heißen diese Adjektive auf Englisch?

1. spektakulär ______________
2. größer ______________
3. der/die/das gruseligste ______________
4. der/die/das modischste ______________
5. wertvoller ______________
6. belebt ______________

11 Hard or easy?

Diese Wörter fand ich in Unit 2 besonders ….

einfach	schwierig
______________	______________
______________	______________
______________	______________
______________	______________

Unit 3 Here we come!

Check-in

coastline ['kəʊstlaɪn]	Küstenlinie
to **travel** ['trævl]	reisen
cliff [klɪf]	Klippe
circle ['sɜ:kl]	Kreis
almost ['ɔ:lməʊst]	fast, beinahe
kilometre ['kɪləʊˌmi:tə; kɪ'lɒmɪtə]	Kilometer
officer ['ɒfɪsə]	Beamter/Beamtin
smuggler ['smʌglə]	Schmuggler/Schmugglerin
to **take** [teɪk]	dauern, (Zeit) brauchen
anywhere ['eniweə]	überall, irgendwo
channel ['tʃænl]	Kanal; Programm
ferry ['feri]	Fähre
to **land** [lænd]	landen
international [ˌɪntə'næʃnl]	international
passenger ['pæsndʒə]	Passagier/Passagierin, Beifahrer/Beifahrerin
port [pɔ:t]	Hafen
cruise [kru:z]	Kreuzfahrt
ocean liner ['əʊʃn ˌlaɪnə]	Ozeandampfer
ocean ['əʊʃn]	Ozean
to **sail** [seɪl]	segeln, fahren (Schiff)
speaker ['spi:kə]	Sprecher/Sprecherin
swimmer ['swɪmə]	Schwimmer/Schwimmerin

Language

lifeguard ['laɪfgɑ:d]	Rettungsschwimmer/ Rettungsschwimmerin
to **fly** [flaɪ]	wehen
sun [sʌn]	Sonne
paradise ['pærəˌdaɪs]	Paradies
on record [ɒn 'rekɔ:d]	verzeichnet, dokumentiert
clean [kli:n]	sauber
sandy ['sændɪ]	sandig

sensible ['sensɪbl]	vernünftig
safe [seɪf]	sicher
to **windsurf** ['wɪndsɜ:f]	windsurfen
to **canoe** [kə'nu:]	Kanu fahren
age [eɪdʒ]	Alter, Zeitalter
bin [bɪn]	Mülleimer, Mülltonne
to **be lost** [bi: 'lɒst]	sich verirrt haben
to **dive** [daɪv]	tauchen
Well done! [ˌwel 'dʌn]	Gut gemacht!
stranger ['streɪndʒə]	Fremder/Fremde
rubber ring [ˌrʌbə 'rɪŋ]	Schwimmreifen
rubber ['rʌbə]	Gummi; Kautschuk
ring [rɪŋ]	Ring
alone [ə'ləʊn]	alleine
stamp [stæmp]	Briefmarke
p.m. [ˌpi:'em]	nachmittags (Uhrzeit)
yard [jɑ:d]	Elle (Längenmaß: 0,914 m)
metre ['mi:tə]	Meter
centimetre ['sentɪˌmi:tə]	Zentimeter
to **notice** ['nəʊtɪs]	bemerken
everyone ['evriwʌn]	jeder
for example [ˌfər‿ɪg'zɑ:mpl]	zum Beispiel
below [bɪ'ləʊ]	unterhalb, unten
Gaelic ['geɪlɪk]	gälisch
Welsh [welʃ]	walisisch; Waliser/Waliserin
Cornish ['kɔ:nɪʃ]	kornisch; aus Cornwall
official [ə'fɪʃl]	offiziell
news (sg.) [nju:z]	Nachricht(en), Neuigkeit(en)
to **signal** ['sɪgnl]	signalisieren, ein Zeichen geben
whose [hu:z]	dessen, deren (Relativpronomen)
mystery ['mɪstri]	Geheimnis, Rätsel
beginning [bɪ'gɪnɪŋ]	Anfang, Beginn
around [ə'raʊnd]	ungefähr, zirka, etwa
wooden ['wʊdn]	hölzern
to **rebuild, rebuilt, rebuilt** [ˌri:'bɪld, ˌri:'bɪlt, ˌri:'bɪlt]	wieder aufbauen; wiederherstellen

ton [tʌn]	Tonne (Gewicht)
to **replace** [rɪˈpleɪs]	ersetzen
up to [ˈʌp tə]	bis zu
way [weɪ]	Art, Weise
to **stand, stood, stood** [stænd, stʊd, stʊd]	stehen
position [pəˈzɪʃn]	Position
exactly [ɪɡˈzæktli]	genau
exact [ɪɡˈzækt]	genau
attraction [əˈtrækʃn]	Attraktion, Sehenswürdigkeit
all over [ˌɔːl‿ˈəʊvə]	überall
a.m. [ˌeɪˈem]	vormittags (Uhrzeit)

Get fit!

to **match** [mætʃ]	passen zu; zuordnen, zusammenfügen
meat [miːt]	Fleisch
passports (pl) [ˈpɑːspɔːts]	Passkontrolle
passport [ˈpɑːspɔːt]	Pass, Reisepass
trolley [ˈtrɒli]	Gepäckwagen, Einkaufwagen, Handkarren
phone box [ˈfəʊn ˌbɒks]	Telefonzelle

Overheard

to **ring, rang, rung** [rɪŋ, ræŋ, rʌŋ]	anrufen

Facts and fiction

announcement [əˈnaʊntsmənt]	Ankündigung, Durchsage
to **trust** [trʌst]	vertrauen
whom [huːm]	wem, wen
mother [ˈmʌðə]	Mutter
father [ˈfɑːðə]	Vater
tug [tʌɡ]	Ziehen, Zupfen
side [saɪd]	Seite
to **take off** [teɪk‿ˈɒf]	ausziehen
to **rest** [rest]	sich entspannen, sich ausruhen

this evening [ðɪs 'i:vnɪŋ]	heute Abend
basement ['beɪsmənt]	Kellergeschoss, Untergeschoss
blind [blaɪnd]	blind
although [ɔ:l'ðəʊ]	obwohl
helpless ['helpləs]	hilflos
independent [ˌɪndɪ'pendənt]	unabhängig
to **lie down** [laɪ 'daʊn]	(sich) hinlegen, niederlegen
to **lie, lay, lain** [laɪ, leɪ, leɪn]	liegen
to **feel for** ['fi:l fə]	tasten nach
no idea [ˌnəʊ‿aɪ'dɪə]	keine Ahnung
stairs (pl) [steəz]	Treppe
footstep ['fʊtstep]	Schritt
both [bəʊθ]	beide
aftershave ['ɑ:ftəʃeɪv]	Aftershave, Rasierwasser
to **get out** [get‿'aʊt]	entkommen
to **touch** [tʌtʃ]	berühren; antippen
fuse-box ['fju:zbɒks]	Sicherungskasten
furious ['fjʊəriəs]	wütend
to **crawl** [krɔ:l]	kriechen, krabbeln
to **grab** [græb]	greifen, schnappen
to **take your chance** [ˌteɪk jɔ: 'tʃɑ:ns]	etwas wagen, etwas riskieren
to **run upstairs** [ˌrʌn‿ʌp'steəz]	die Treppe hinaufrennen
to **lock** [lɒk]	abschließen
icon ['aɪkɒn]	Ikone
would [wʊd]	würde(n)
to **be wrong** [bi: 'rɒŋ]	Unrecht haben
to **understand, understood, understood** [ˌʌndə'stænd, ˌʌndə'stʊd,ˌ ʌndə'stʊd]	verstehen

Wordwise

European [jʊərə'pi:ən]	europäisch

Check-out

engine ['endʒɪn]	Maschine, Motor
loch [lɒx]	See (schottisch)
lake [leɪk]	See

1 Words for pictures

Finde die richtigen Wörter zu den Bildern.

1. ______________________________

2. ______________________________

3. ______________________________

4. ______________________________

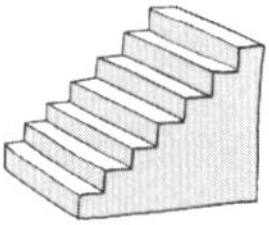

5. ______________________________

2 Weights and measurements

Schreibe auf Englisch alle Maße und Gewichtseinheiten auf, die dir einfallen.

____

____

____

3 Little words

Wie heißen die kleinen Wörter?

1. fast ______________
2. irgendwo ______________
3. jeder ______________
4. dessen, deren ______________
5. bis zu ______________

4 Wordsnake

Welche Wörter sind in der Wortschlange versteckt? Finde sie und schreibe sie auf.

____

____

____

____

5 Odd one out

Welches Wort fällt aus der Reihe?

1.	cruise	ocean liner	stranger
2	kilometre	yard	meat
3.	to sail	lake	to windsurf
4.	everyone	mother	father
5	Gaelic	Welsh	aftershave
6.	loch	fuse-box	lake

6 Irregular verbs

Vervollständige die Tabelle.

to take		
	rebuilt	
		stood
to lie		
	felt	
		got
	ran	
to understand		

7 Opposites

Finde das Gegenteil.

1. national ______________
2. moon ______________
3. dirty ______________
4. together ______________

8 One word or two?

Setze die Wörter richtig zusammen. Achte darauf, ob sie getrennt oder zusammen geschrieben werden.

coast	ocean	any	box	where	ring
life	rubber	phone	liner	line	guard

______________ ______________

______________ ______________

______________ ______________

9 German and English words

Setze die englischen Wörter ein. Unterstreiche die Unterschiede zwischen den deutschen und englischen Wörtern.

1. ______________________ – Ozean
2. ______________________ = sandig
3. ______________________ = Kilometer
4. ______________________ = Kanal
5. ______________________ = Schwimmer
6. ______________________ = Paradies
7. ______________________ = Beginn
8. ______________________ = Ikone

10 Verbs

Verbinde die Wörter richtig.

1. to take	for
2. to feel	off
3. to run	down
4. to get	lost
5. to lie	upstairs
6. to be	out

Unit 4 Let it out!

Check-in

to **let, let, let** [let, let, let]	lassen
tattoo [tæt'u:]	Tätowierung
disappointed [ˌdɪsə'pɔɪntɪd]	enttäuscht
frustrated [frʌs'treɪtɪd]	frustriert
strict [strɪkt]	streng, strikt
to **have an argument** [ˌhæv‿ən‿'ɑ:gjəmənt]	sich streiten
argument ['ɑ:gjəmənt]	Streit; Argument
I want my ... pierced. [aɪ 'wɒnt maɪ ... 'pɪəst]	Ich möchte mein ... piercen lassen.
to **want sb to do sth** [wɒnt]	wollen, dass jemand etwas tut
eyebrow ['aɪbraʊ]	Augenbraue
tongue [tʌŋ]	Zunge
direct [dɪ'rekt]	direkt
respect [rɪ'spekt]	Respekt
poetry slam ['pəʊətri ˌslæm]	Poetry Slam (Gedichtwettbewerb)
poetry ['pəʊətri]	Lyrik
year-old [ˌjɪər‿'əʊld]	-jährig; -Jähriger/-Jährige
winner ['wɪnə]	Gewinner/Gewinnerin, Sieger/Siegerin
to **take part in** [teɪk 'pɑ:t‿ɪn]	teilnehmen an
workshop ['wɜ:kʃɒp]	Workshop, Werkstatt
performance [pə'fɔ:məns]	Aufführung, Vorstellung
to **take place** [teɪk 'pleɪs]	stattfinden
poet ['pəʊɪt]	Dichter/Dichterin, Poet/Poetin
to **invent** [ɪn'vent]	erfinden
live [laɪv]	live
teenage ['ti:neɪdʒ]	jugendlich
poem ['pəʊɪm]	Gedicht
wish [wɪʃ]	Wunsch
boyfriend ['bɔɪfrend]	Freund (in einer Paarbeziehung)

special ['speʃl]	besonders, speziell
to **perform** [pə'fɔ:m]	aufführen, auftreten
in all [ɪn‿'ɔ:l]	insgesamt, im Ganzen
organizer ['ɔ:gənaɪzə]	Organisator/Organisatorin, Veranstalter/Veranstalterin
audience ['ɔ:diəns]	Publikum
slamster ['slæmstə]	Teilnehmer/Teilnehmerin an einem Poetry Slam
each [i:tʃ]	je, jeweils
content ['kɒntent]	Inhalt
response [rɪ'spɒns]	Reaktion, Antwort

Language

diary ['daɪəri]	Tagebuch; Terminkalender
disaster [dɪ'zɑ:stə]	Desaster, Katastrophe
village ['vɪlɪdʒ]	Dorf
cottage ['kɒtɪdʒ]	kleines Landhaus, Ferienhaus
middle ['mɪdl]	Mitte; Mittel-
nowhere ['nəʊweə]	nirgendwo, nirgendwohin
not even [nɒt‿'i:vn]	nicht einmal
to **hang out, hung out, hung out** [hæŋ‿'aʊt, hʌŋ‿'aʊt, hʌŋ‿'aʊt]	sich herumtreiben
steel band [ˌsti:l 'bænd]	Steelband (Band, deren Instrumente aus leeren Ölfässern bestehen)
to **upset, upset, upset** [ʌp'set, ʌp'set, ʌp'set]	erschrecken, durcheinander bringen; umstoßen
feeling ['fi:lɪŋ]	Gefühl
useless ['ju:sləs]	nutzlos
to **text** [tekst]	Textnachricht (SMS) schicken, simsen
to **put out** [pʊt‿'aʊt]	hinausstellen
suggestion [sə'dʒestʃn]	Vorschlag, Anregung
shall [ʃæl]	sollen
to **get off** [get‿'ɒf]	wegräumen von, abräumen von

comprehensive school [kɒmprɪ'hensɪv ˌsku:l]	Gesamtschule
survival [sə'vaɪvl]	Überleben
notice board ['nəʊtɪs bɔ:d]	schwarzes Brett
notice ['nəʊtɪs]	Anschlag, Notiz
vending machine ['vendɪŋ məˌʃi:n]	Warenautomat
machine [mə'ʃi:n]	Maschine, Apparat
leaflet ['li:flət]	Flugblatt, Prospekt
to **guess** [ges]	raten, vermuten
yukky ['jʌki]	ekelhaft
session ['seʃnv]	Veranstaltung
as soon as [əz 'su:n‿əz]	sobald
shy [ʃaɪ]	schüchtern
mirror ['mɪrə]	Spiegel
to **scare** ['skeə]	erschrecken, einen Schrecken einjagen, Angst machen
abroad [ə'brɔ:d]	im/ins Ausland
Welcome to ... ['welkəm tə]	Willkommen in ...
to **compare** [kəm'peə]	vergleichen
system ['sɪstəm]	System
compulsory [kəm'pʌlsri]	obligatorisch, zwingend
of age [əv‿'eɪdʒ]	im Alter von
state [steɪt]	Staat, Land; staatlich; Zustand
as well as [əz 'wel‿əz]	sowohl … als auch
private ['praɪvɪt]	privat
following ['fɒləʊɪŋ]	folgend/folgender/folgende/folgendes
grid [grɪd]	Gitter, Tabelle
primary school ['praɪməri ˌsku:l]	Grundschule
grammar school ['græmə ˌsku:l]	Gymnasium
exam [ɪg'zæm]	Examen, Prüfung
GCSE [ˌdʒi:si:es'i:]	Prüfung zum Abschluss der Sekundarstufe

A-levels (pl) ['eɪlevlz]	brit. Abitur
possible ['pɒsəbl]	möglich
college ['kɒlɪdʒ]	College; Institut
advanced [əd'vɑːnst]	fortgeschritten
level ['levl]	Ebene, Niveau

Get fit!

glad [glæd]	froh
to **put in** [pʊt‿'ɪn]	einschieben
extra ['ekstrə]	zusätzlich; Zusatz
training ['treɪnɪŋ]	Training, Ausbildung
lots of love [ˌlɒts‿əv 'lʌv]	viele Grüße (am Briefende)
to **wish** [wɪʃ]	wünschen
proud of ['praʊd‿əv]	stolz auf
to **make it** ['meɪk‿ɪt]	es schaffen
to **jump about** [ˌdʒʌmp‿ə'baʊt]	herumspringen
winning goal ['wɪnɪŋ gəʊl]	Siegtreffer

Overheard

to **fight, fought, fought** [faɪt, fɔːt, fɔːt]	streiten, kämpfen
to **stay out** [steɪ‿'aʊt]	wegbleiben
to **advise** [əd'vaɪz]	raten
answerphone ['ɑːnsəfəʊn]	Anrufbeantworter
to **suggest** [sə'dʒest]	vorschlagen
It's ... speaking. [ɪts ... 'spiːkɪŋ]	Hier spricht ... .

Facts and fiction

choice [tʃɔɪs]	Wahl, Auswahl
fuss [fʌs]	Aufregung, Wirbel
you'd better [jʊd 'betə]	du solltest lieber
sudden ['sʌdn]	plötzlich
glare [gleə]	blendender Glanz, grelles Licht
What the heck ... ? [ˌwɒt ðə 'hek]	Was zum Teufel ... ?

such [sʌtʃ]	solch
wreck [rek]	Wrack
to **try hard** [traɪ‿'hɑ:d]	sich stark bemühen
lead [led]	Blei
stroke [strəʊk]	Schlag(anfall)
harm [hɑ:m]	Schaden, Verletzung
dear [dɪə]	Schatz (Anrede)
to **have a fit** [ˌhæv‿ə 'fɪt]	einen Anfall bekommen, Zustände kriegen
to **care** [keə]	sich kümmern, sich interessieren, wichtig nehmen
to **get into such a state** [get‿ˌɪntə 'sʌtʃ‿ə 'steɪt]	durchdrehen, (sich) verrückt machen
to **the brink** [tə ðə 'brɪŋk]	an den Rand, bis zur Oberkante
to **swerve** [swɜ:v]	ausweichen, ausscheren
curve [kɜ:v]	Kurve
alive [ə'laɪv]	lebendig
to **shake, shook, shaken** [ʃeɪk, ʃʊk, 'ʃeɪkn]	schütteln, zittern
leaf, leaves (pl) [li:f; li:vz]	Blatt
wave [weɪv]	Welle
to **go weak** [gəʊ 'wi:k]	schwach werden
weak [wi:k]	schwach
to **choke** [tʃəʊk]	ersticken
glee [gli:]	Entzücken

1 Poetry Slam

Ergänze die fehlenden Buchstaben.

1. y__a__-__ld
2. w__nn__r
3. __nv__nt
4. t__en__ge
5. p__et__y
6. w__rk__h__p
7. sl__m__ter
8. p__rf__rm

2 Irregular verbs

Ergänze die Tabelle.

to let		
	hung out	
		upset
	got off	
to put out		
		fought
	shook	
to go		

3 Adjectives

In dieser Unit hast du viele neue Adjektive gelernt. Schreibe alle auf, die dir einfallen.

____

____

____

4 Small words

Wo kommen die kleinen Wörter hin?

off place out out about out

1. to take ____________
2. to hang ____________
3. to get ____________
4. to jump ____________
5. to put ____________
6. to stay ____________

5 Reflexive pronouns

Ergänze die Reflexivpronomen.

1. I wash ______________________
2. You dress ______________________
3. He feeds ______________________
4. She scares ______________________
5. It explains ______________________
6. We enjoy ______________________
7. You all love ______________________

6 Odd one out

Welches Wort fällt aus der Reihe?

1.	A-levels	GCSE	mirror	exam
2.	girlfriend	love	boyfriend	session
3.	poet	poetry	wish	poem
4.	tattoo	pierced	tongue	village
5.	school	private	university	college

7 Wordsnake

Welche Wörter sind in der Wortschlange versteckt?

____

____

8 What can you say?

Wie sagst du das auf Englisch?

1. Was zum Teufel…?

____

2. Du willst einen Brief mit “Viele Grüße” beenden.

____

3. Du meldest dich am Telefon mit deinem Namen.

____

9 Words for pictures

Finde die richtigen Wörter zu den Bildern.

1. ______________________

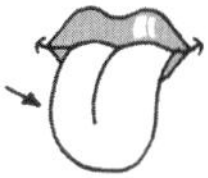

2. ______________________

3. ______________________

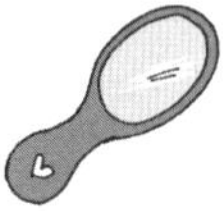

4. ______________________

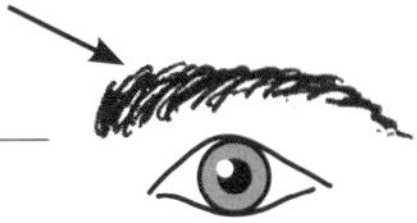

5. ______________________

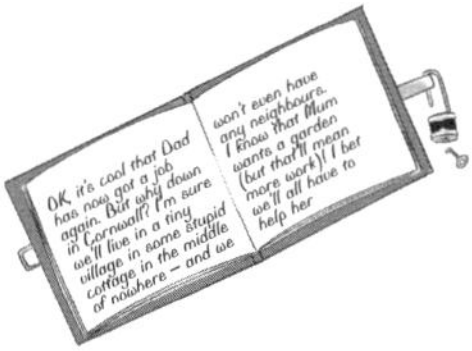

6. ______________________

10 English or German?

Welche englischen Wörter aus Unit 4 werden ähnlich geschrieben wie im Deutschen? Schreibe fünf auf und unterstreiche die Unterschiede.

German	English

11 Poetry slam

Was gehört alles zu einem Poetry Slam?

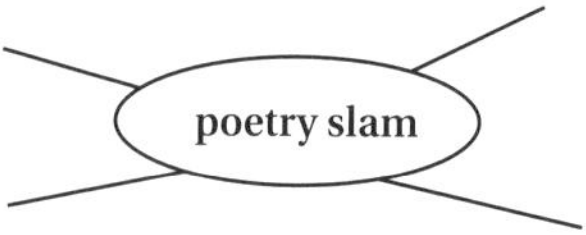

12 New words

Diese Wörter fand ich in Unit 4 besonders …

schwer zu merken	leicht zu merken	nützlich

Unit 5 Screen shots

Check-in

screen shot ['skriːn ˌʃɒt]	Screenshot
screen [skriːn]	Bildschirm, Leinwand
shot [ʃɒt]	Schuss, Schlag
programme ['prəʊgræm]	Programm, Sendung
tough [tʌf]	hart, rau, zäh
fair [feə]	blond, hell
heroine ['herəʊɪn]	Heldin
average ['ævrɪdʒ]	durchschnittlich
daily ['deɪli]	täglich
talk show ['tɔːk ˌʃəʊ]	Talkshow
reality show [ri'æləti ˌʃəʊ]	Realityshow
viewer ['vjuːə]	Zuschauer/Zuschauerin
per [pɜː]	pro
industry ['ɪndəstri]	Industrie
twice [twaɪs]	zweimal
musical ['mjuːzɪkl]	Musical
success [sək'ses]	Erfolg
catchy ['kætʃi]	eingängig
colourful ['kʌləfl]	bunt, farbig
dramatic [drə'mætɪk]	dramatisch
scene [siːn]	Szene, Schauplatz
in contrast to [ɪn 'kɒntrɑːst tə]	im Gegensatz zu
contrast ['kɒntrɑːst]	Kontrast, Gegensatz
seldom ['seldəm]	selten
to **kiss** [kɪs]	küssen
cartoon [kɑː'tuːn]	Cartoon, Zeichentrickfilm
comedy ['kɒmədi]	Komödie
detective story [dɪ'tektɪv ˌstɔːri]	Krimi
documentary [ˌdɒkjə'mentri]	Dokumentarfilm
docu soap ['dɒkju ˌsəʊp]	Dokusoap
science fiction [ˌsaɪəns 'fɪkʃn]	Sciencefiction
fiction ['fɪkʃn]	Erfindung, Fiktion
thriller ['θrɪlə]	Thriller
myth [mɪθ]	Mythos

grave [greɪv]	Grab
script [skrɪpt]	Drehbuch
to **go (together) with** ['gəʊ wɪð]	passen zu

Language

pet [pet]	Haustier, Liebling
final ['faɪnl]	letzte/letzter/letztes
seaside ['si:saɪd]	Küste, Meeresküste
rescue ['reskju:]	Rettung
cook [kʊk]	Koch/Köchin
link [lɪŋk]	Verbindung, Bindeglied
host [həʊst]	Gastgeber, Talkmaster
charts (pl) [tʃɑ:ts]	Charts, Hitparade
hit [hɪt]	Hit
series, series (pl) ['sɪəri:z]	Serie
hound [haʊnd]	Jagdhund
sitcom ['sɪtkɒm]	Situationskomödie
alien ['eɪliən]	Fremder/Fremde, Außerirdischer/Außerirdische
diamond ['daɪəmənd]	Diamant
jewellery ['dʒu:əlri]	Schmuck
countdown ['kaʊntdaʊn]	Countdown
emergency [ɪ'mɜ:dʒnsi]	Notfall, Notlage
patient ['peɪʃnt]	Patient/Patientin
travel ['trævl]	Reise
on the job [ˌɒn ðə 'dʒɒb]	bei der Arbeit
runaway ['rʌnəˌweɪ]	Ausreißer/Ausreißerin
anybody ['eniˌbɒdi]	irgendjemand, jeder (beliebige)
lad [læd]	Junge
somebody ['sʌmbədi]	jemand
He had something on his mind. [maɪnd]	Ihn beschäftigte etwas.
mind [maɪnd]	Geist, Verstand
perhaps [pə'hæps]	vielleicht
hotel [həʊ'tel]	Hotel
safe [seɪf]	Safe, Tresor

to **attack** [əˈtæk]	angreifen
inspector [ɪnˈspektə]	Inspektor
crime [kraɪm]	Verbrechen; Kriminalität
suspect [ˈsʌspekt]	Verdächtigter/Verdächtigte
to **smoke** [sməʊk]	rauchen
pipe [paɪp]	Pfeife
reception [rɪˈsepʃn]	Rezeption, Empfang
downstairs [ˌdaʊnˈsteəz]	(die Treppe) hinunter/herunter
upstairs [ʌpˈsteəz]	(die Treppe) hinauf/herauf
receptionist [rɪˈsepʃnɪst]	Empfangschef/Empfangschefin
to **pass** [pɑːs]	vorbeigehen an
nobody [ˈnəʊbədi]	niemand
guard [gɑːd]	Wache; Wächter/Wächerin
ladder [ˈlædə]	Leiter
while [waɪl]	während
to **pay, paid, paid** [peɪ, peɪd, peɪd]	(be)zahlen
guest [gest]	Gast

Get fit!

son [sʌn]	Sohn
mistake [mɪˈsteɪk]	Fehler
called [kɔːld]	genannt
brave [breɪv]	tapfer, mutig
wife, wives (pl) [waɪf; waɪvz]	Ehefrau
hunting [ˈhʌntɪŋ]	Jagen
to **get on** [get‿ˈɒn]	aufsteigen, einsteigen (in Zug, Bus ...)
to open [ˈəʊpn]	sich öffnen, aufgehen
to turn [tɜːn]	drehen, sich umdrehen
strong [strɒŋ]	stark
wolf, wolves (pl) [wʊlf; wʊlvz]	Wolf
tooth, teeth (pl) [tuːθ; tiːθ]	Zahn
blood [blʌd]	Blut
cry [kraɪ]	Schrei
hurt [hɜːt]	verletzt

dead [ded]	tot
shocked [ʃɒkt]	geschockt, schockiert
to **bury** ['beri]	begraben, beerdigen
gravestone ['greɪvstəʊn]	Grabstein

Overheard

to **walk up to** [wɔ:k‿'ʌp tə]	hingehen, zugehen auf
director [dɪ'rektə]	Direktor/Direktorin, Regisseur/Regisseurin
assistant [ə'sɪstnt]	Assistent/Assistentin
to **film** [fɪlm]	filmen
secret ['si:krət]	Geheimnis

Facts and fiction

to **murder** ['mɜ:də]	ermorden
to **glow** [gləʊ]	leuchten
dark [dɑ:k]	Dunkelheit
only ['əʊnli]	einzige/einziger/einziges
inheritor [ɪn'herɪtə]	Erbe/Erbin
nephew ['nefju:]	Neffe
What's the matter? [ˌwɒts ðə 'mætə]	Was ist los?
to **solve** [sɒlv]	lösen
trust [trʌst]	Vertrauen
to **agree** [ə'gri:]	zustimmen, einer Meinung sein
poor [pɔ:; pʊə]	arm
boot [bu:t]	Stiefel
beard [bɪəd]	Bart
servant ['sɜ:vnt]	Diener/Dienerin
barking ['bɑ:kɪŋ]	Bellen
sense [sens]	Sinn, Bedeutung
smell [smel]	Geruch, Gestank
to **go for a walk** [ˌgəʊ fər‿ə 'wɔ:k]	spazieren gehen
to **sound** [saʊnd]	klingen, sich anhören
absolutely [ˌæbsə'lu:tli]	absolut, völlig

grey [greɪ]	grau
scientist ['saɪəntɪst]	Wissenschaftler/Wissenschaftlerin
painting ['peɪntɪŋ]	Gemälde
fireplace ['faɪəpleɪs]	Kamin
powder ['paʊdə]	Puder, Pulver
to **knock** [nɒk]	klopfen; stoßen, schlagen
close [kləʊs]	nahe
to **share** [ʃeə]	teilen
size [saɪz]	Größe, Kleidergröße
to **sniff** [snɪf]	schnüffeln, schnuppern
enormous [ɪ'nɔ:məs]	enorm, riesig
body ['bɒdi]	Körper
towards [tə'wɔ:dz]	in Richtung, auf … zu, darauf zu
gunshot ['gʌnʃɒt]	Schuss
to **echo** ['ekəʊ]	widerhallen
gun [gʌn]	Schusswaffe
to **arrest** [ə'rest]	festnehmen, verhaften

1 Mixed words

Welche Verben verstecken sich in diesem Buchstabensalat?

1. tatakc → ______________________________
2. ekoms → ______________________________
3. unrt → ______________________________
4. rdumre → ______________________________
5. wglo → ______________________________
6. ffsin → ______________________________

2 Words for pictures

Finde die richtigen Wörter zu den Bildern.

1. ______________________

2. ______________________

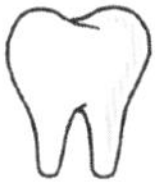

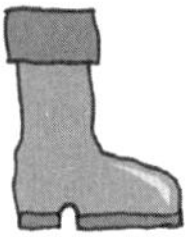

3. ______________________

4. ______________________

5. ______________________

3 Little words

Wie heißen die kleinen Wörter?

1. pro ______________________
2. selten ______________________
3. während ______________________
4. zweimal ______________________
5. vielleicht ______________________

4 Odd one out

Welches Wort fällt aus der Reihe?

1.	comedy	science fiction	thriller	heroine
2.	director	hound	assistant	viewer
3.	inspector	crime	sitcom	suspect
4.	dead	gravestone	painting	to bury
5.	nephew	son	wife	servant

5 Who or what is it?

Welche Wörter werden hier gesucht?

1. Who tries to solve crimes? ____________________
2. Who lies in hospital? ____________________
3. Someone who you invite to your house.

   ____
4. Another word for 'maybe'. ____________________

6 Opposites

Finde das Gegenteil.

1. alive ____________________
2. daughter ____________________
3. to close ____________________
4. upstairs ____________________

7 Who am I?

Finde die richtigen Buchstaben.

1. The first letter of 'suspect'. ____
2. The second letter of 'script'. ____
3. The second and fifth letter of 'fiction'. ____
4. The fourth and fifth letter of 'screen'. ____
5. The last letter of 'reception'. ____
6. The second and third letter of 'attack'. ____
7. The third letter of 'alien'. ____
8. The last letter of 'towards'. ____
9. The last letter of 'arrest'. ____
10. I do a lot of experiments. ________________________

8 Word groups

Sortiere die Wörter in die richtigen Themenbereiche.

to murder, hotel, crime, safe, receptionist, dead, inspector, blood, waiter, room, to solve, to arrest

a detective story	**at the hotel**
________________	________________
________________	________________
________________	________________
________________	________________

9 Word puzzle

Finde die 13 Wörter im Puzzle. Sie sind senkrecht, waagerecht und diagonal versteckt.

brave, comedy, director, documentary, dramatic, guard, hero, heroine, musical, pipe, son, viewer, wife

D	N	H	E	R	O	I	N	E
O	C	P	F	N	D	V	N	D
C	J	O	J	P	I	P	E	U
U	D	H	M	E	I	S	A	H
M	H	T	W	E	G	S	G	F
E	K	E	R	U	D	T	H	E
N	R	W	A	E	R	Y	J	H
T	W	R	K	B	E	G	S	E
A	D	I	R	E	C	T	O	R
R	R	A	F	I	Z	U	N	O
Y	V	W	E	E	Z	T	Z	K
E	D	R	A	M	A	T	I	C
L	K	W	J	P	W	H	Z	G
J	M	U	S	I	C	A	L	T

10 What's the word?

Wie heißen diese Wörter auf Englisch?

1. [sək'ses] ________________
2. ['nəʊbədi] ________________
3. [mɪ'steɪk] ________________
4. [haʊnd] ________________
5. [kʊk] ________________
6. [ʃɒkt] ________________

Lösungen

Unit 1

1 1. rugby 2. player 3. competition 4. stadium 5. pitch 6. goalkeeper 7. back line 8. referee

2 1. American football 2. rugby boot 3. back line 4. couch potato 5. swimming pool 6. home plate 7. goal post

3 Vorschlag: pitch, helmet, glove, bat, ball, home plate, pitcher, batter, catcher, player

4 1. cup 2. doorstep 3. whistle 4. inch 5. stand 6. birth 7. net 8. fair

5 at the top, at the bottom, at the front, at the back

6 1. during 2. you/they 3. against 4. nearly 5. enough 6. across

7 1. at the bottom 2. full 3. ancient 4. at the back

8 1. foot 2. couch 3. cup 4. helmet 5. gloves

9 1. cups 2. centuries 3. pitches 4. feet 5. couch potatoes 6. bosses

10 [əʊ]: row, post, lonely, home, stone; [ɒ]: across, knock; [ɔ:]: score, born; [ʌ]: glove

11 1. catcher 2. batter 3. singer 4. player 5. teacher 6. reporter

12 Vorschlag: to catch, to bat, to score, to kill, to cycle, to send off

13 Schülerlösung

Unit 2

1 1. spectacular 2. trendy 3. rich 4. expensive 5. scary

2

R	F	D	J	J	S	N	O	N	R
M	O	A	R	E	W	E	C	T	E
F	R	Y	K	W	F	W	O	P	G
C	L	F	A	E	B	S	U	R	U
T	A	X	I	L	U	P	R	I	L
H	S	I	N	C	E	A	I	N	A
B	U	S	Y	L	U	P	E	C	R
I	A	G	A	F	T	E	R	E	K
F	S	K	E	E	T	R	F	G	N
A	D	C	H	F	J	E	N	T	D
S	D	L	C	Q	U	E	U	E	H
F	I	N	A	L	L	Y	E	R	L

3 1. underground 2. teenager 3. to enter 4. capsule 5. sauerkraut

4 Vorschlag: museum, fortress, palace, department store, castle, tower, prison, menagerie, house, church, school, hospital

5 to go far, to give up, to come true, to put out, to get interested

6 1. building 2. deliver 3. pollution 4. milkman 5. tradition 6. monastery 7. straw 8. fortress

7 1. scariest 2. best 3. faster 4. trendiest 5. oldest

8 1. view 2. relive 3. underground 4. pickpocket

9 1. inside 2. after 3. quarter 4. finally 5. since

10 1. spectacular 2. bigger 3. the scariest 4. the trendiest 5. more valuable 6. busy

11 Schülerlösung

Unit 3

1 1. sun 2. rubber ring 3. ring 4. stamp 5. stairs

2 Vorschlag: mile, inch, foot, yard, kilometre, pound, stone, gramme

3 1. almost 2. somewhere 3. everybody 4. whose 5. up to

4 travel, kilometre, passport, trolley, international, passenger, fly, European, announcement, officer, channel, ferry, land, port

5 1. stranger 2. meat 3. lake 4. everyone 5. aftershave 6. fuse-box

6 to take – took – taken, to rebuild – rebuilt – rebuilt,
to stand – stood – stood, to lie – lay – lain,
to feel – felt – felt, to get – got – got, to run – ran – run,
to understand – understood – understood

7 1. international 2. sun 3. clean 4. alone

8 lifeguard, ocean liner, coastline, anywhere, phone box, rubber ring

9 1. ocean – Ozean
2. sandy – sandig
3. kilometre – Kilometer
4. channel – Kanal
5. swimmer – Schwimmer
6. paradise – Paradies

7. beginning – Beginn
8. icon – Ikone

10 1. to take off 2. to feel for 3. to run upstairs 4. to get out 5. to lie down 6. to be lost

Unit 4

1 1. year-old 2. winner 3. to invent 4. teenage 5. poetry 6. workshop 5. slamster 7. perform

2 to let – let – let, to hang out – hung out – hung out, to upset – upset – upset, to get off – got off – got off, to put out – put out – put out, to fight – fought – fought, to shake – shook – shaken, to go - went – gone

3 Vorschlag: disappointed, frustrated, strict, direct, useless, shy, compulsory, private, glad, proud, alive, weak

4 1. to take place 2, to hang out 3. to get off 4. to jump about 5. to put out 6. to stay out

5 1. myself 2. yourself 3. himself 4. herself 5. itself 6. ourselves 7. yourselves

6 1. mirror 2. session 3. wish 4. village 5. private

7 disaster, useless, argument, content, response, village, nowhere, feeling, possible, suggest, choice

8 1. What the heck ... ? 2. lots of love 3. Hello, it's ... speaking.

9 1. tongue 2. wave 3. mirror 4. leaf 5. eyebrow 6. diary

10 Vorschlag:
Gewinner – winner
direkt – direct
speziell – special
Desaster – disaster
Notiz – notice

11 Vorschlag: poetry, poem, judge, slamster, slam rule, winner, round, take part, enter, workshop, performance, poet, perform, audience

12 Schülerlösung